Where Do They Live?

Animals Around the World

Written and
illustrated
by
Anne Corsmeier

ISBN 979-8-9902724-4-6

To my students

Let's take a trip
around the world
and see where
some animals
live.

This is Africa.

Africa is a continent.

Let's look at some
animals that live in
Africa.

Lions can be
found in Africa.

Elephants can be
found in Africa.

Zebras can be
found in Africa.

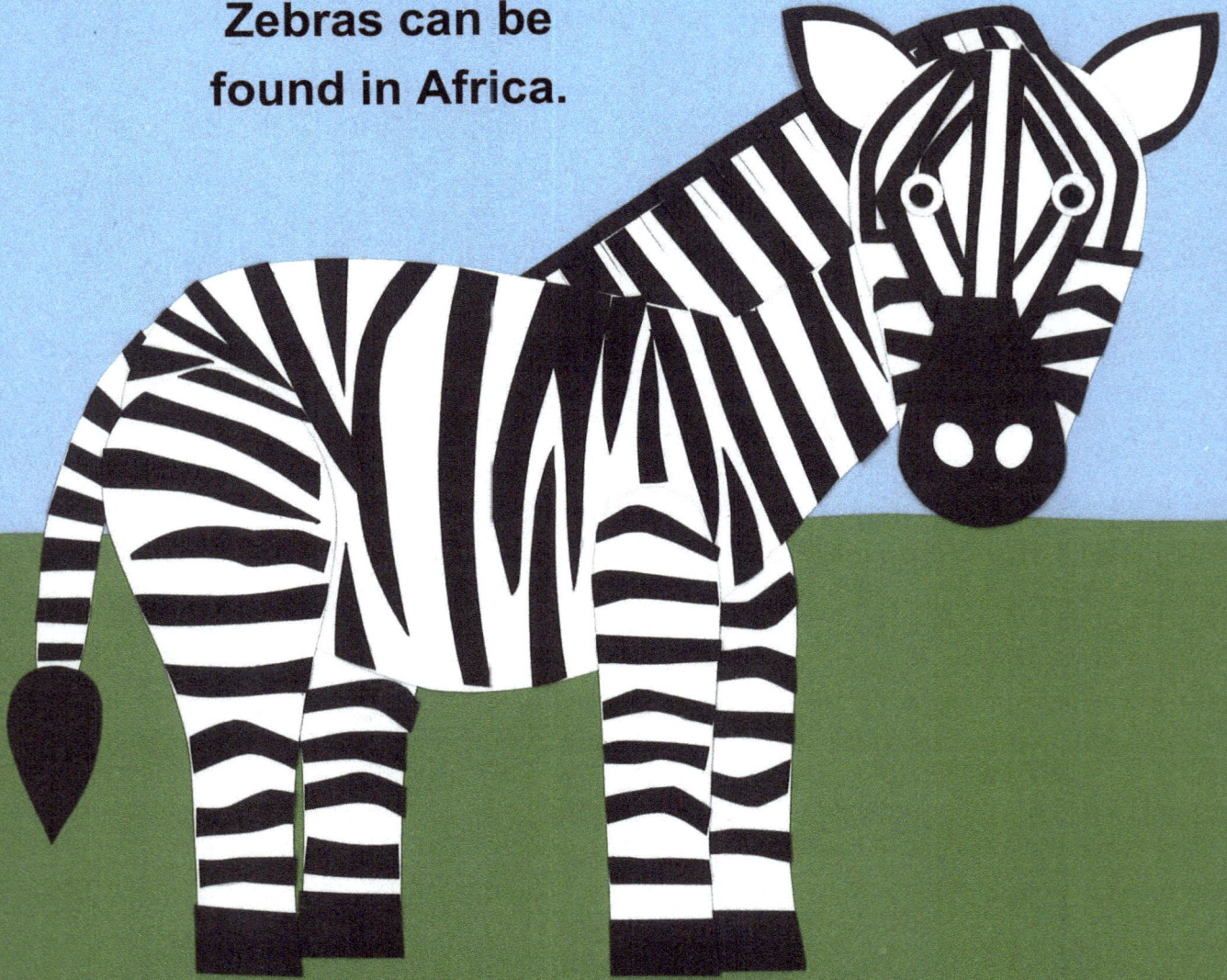

Giraffes can be
found in Africa.

This is Europe.
Europe is a continent.
Let's look at some
animals that live in
Europe.

Badgers can be
found in Europe.

Red foxes can be
found in Europe.

This is Asia.
Asia is a continent.
Let's look at some
animals that live in
Asia.

Pandas can be
found in Asia.

Tigers can be
found in Asia.

This is Australia.
Australia is a continent.
Let's look at some
animals that live in
Australia.

Koalas can be
found in Australia.

Kangaroos can be
found in Australia.

This is Antarctica.
Antarctica is a continent.
Let's look at some
animals that live in
Antarctica.

Penguins can
be found in
Antarctica.

Leopard seals
can be found
in Antarctica.

This is South America.
South America is a continent.
Let's look at some
animals that live in
South America.

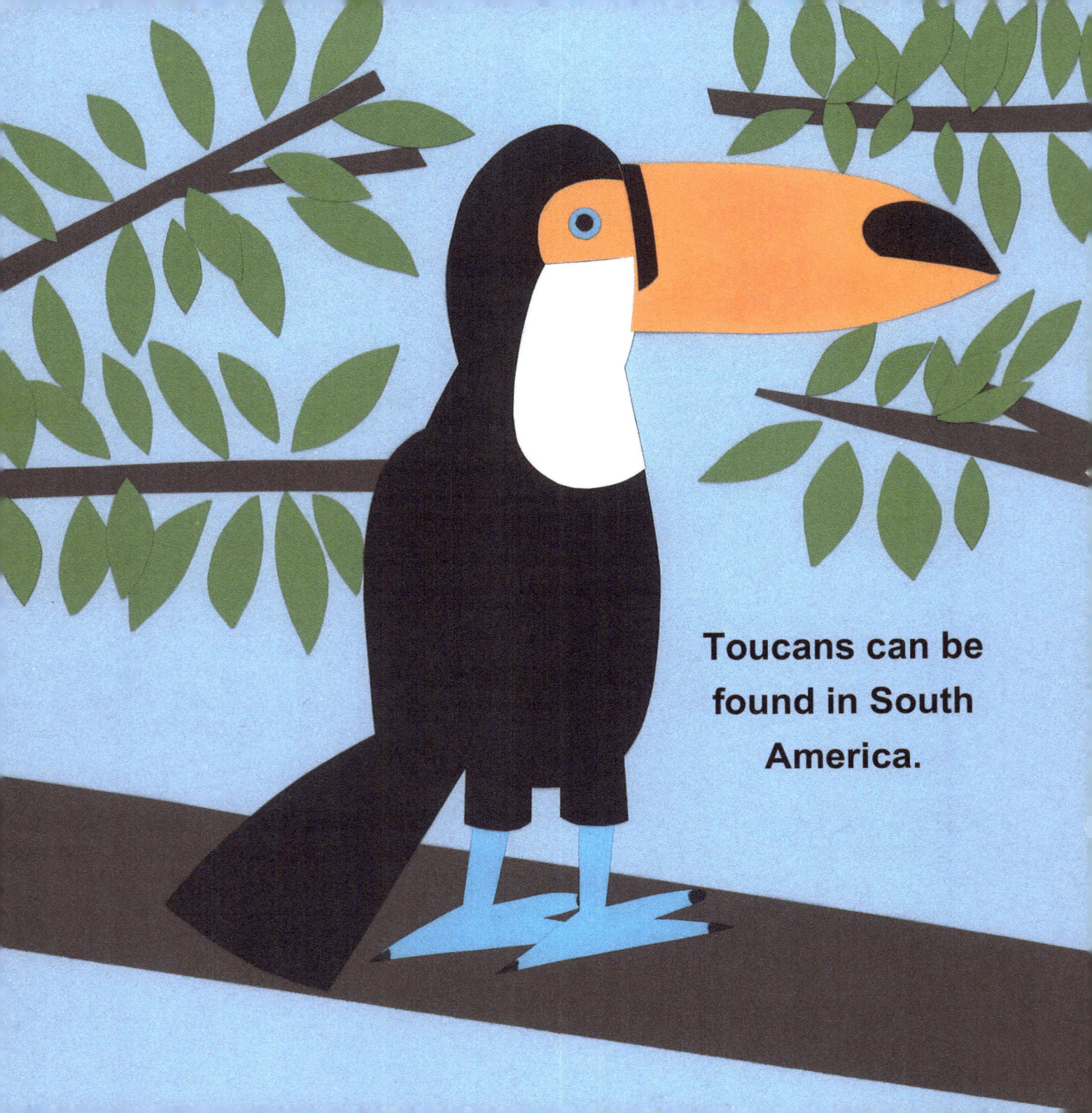

Toucans can be found in South America.

Red-eyed tree frogs
can be found in
South America.

Sloths can be found in
South America.

Jaguars can be found
in South America.

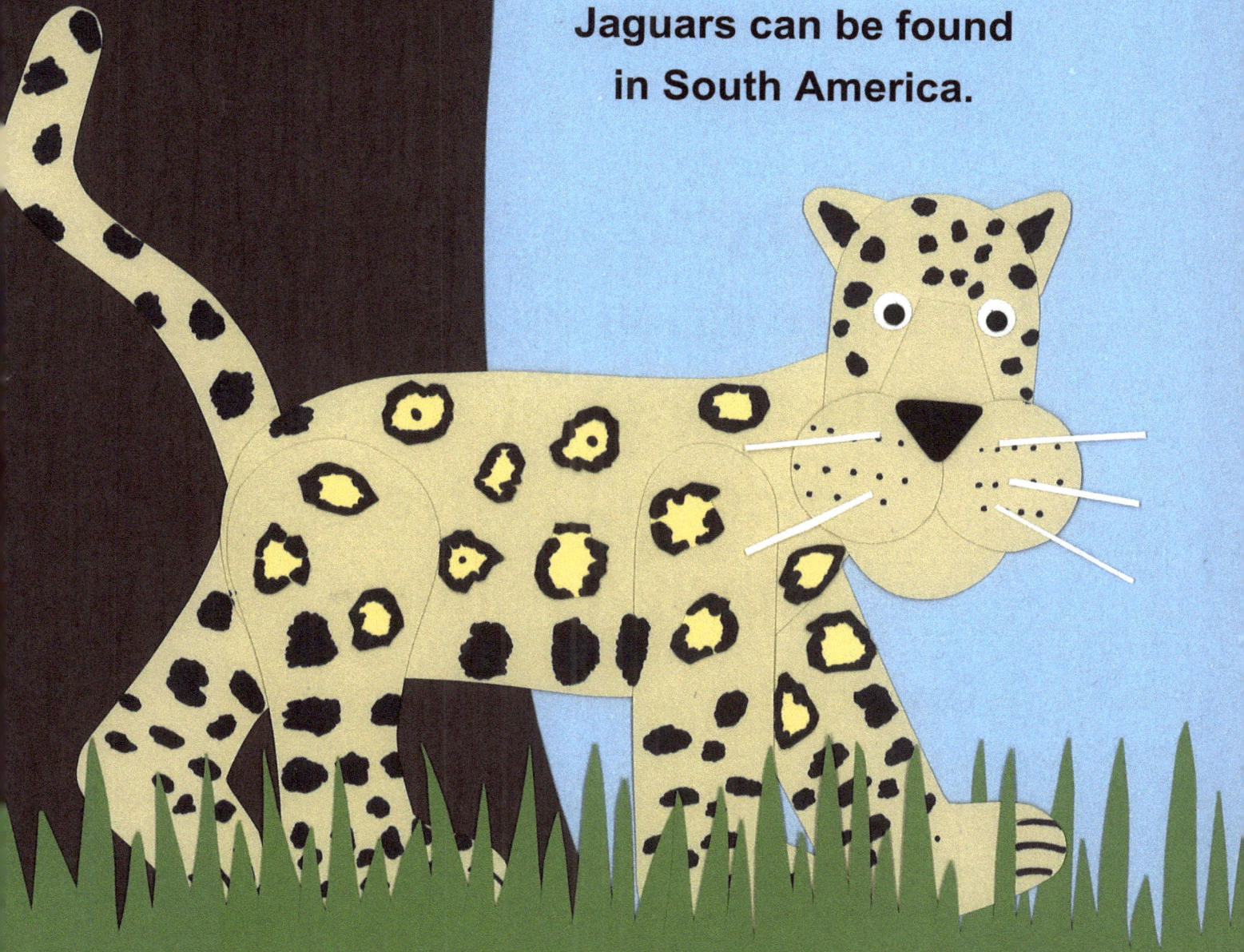

This is North America.
North America is a continent.
Let's look at some
animals that live in
North America.

Beavers can be
found in
North America.

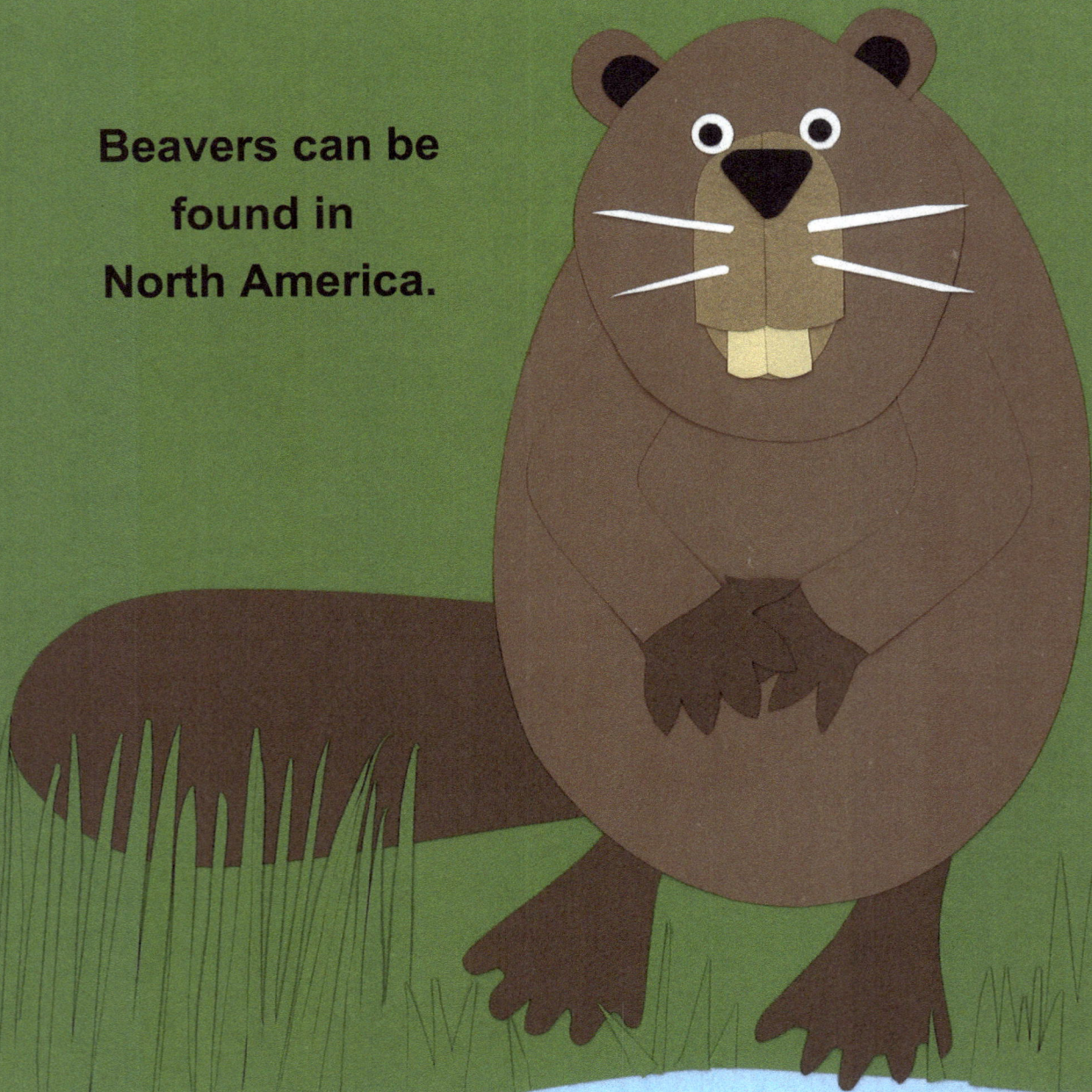

Alligators can be found
in North America.

Can you match each animal to its continent?

www.ingramcontent.com/pod-product-compliance
Lightning Source LLC
Chambersburg PA
CBHW041636040426
42448CB00023B/3493